MADE Marvelous

written by Adree Williams
illustrated by Jamie Cosley

This book is dedicated to our beautiful daughter.

Written by Adree Williams
Illustrated by Jamie Cosley
Published by Marvelous Works Publications

All rights reserved. No part of this book may be reproduced or transmitted in any form or by any means, electronic or mechanical, including photocopying, recording, or by an information storage or retrieval system-except by a reviewer who may quote brief passages in a review to be printed in a magazine or newspaper-without permission in writing from the publisher.

Copyright © 2019 by Adree Williams
Hardcover ISBN 978-1-7333120-1-1
Paperback ISBN 978-1-7333120-4-2

Meet Rose who has a special story to share.
She hopes to remind others to be kind
and show that they care.

Rose has three older brothers who are simply the best. They are fun, have great hearts, and are always looking for a new quest.

They each are made marvelous in their own special ways. This gives them different interests in how they spend their days.

Randy is creative and a cowboy at heart.
Miles is sweet, tender and smart.
Fisher is tough, funny and full of might.

And Rose is the princess with a sparkle so bright!

Rose was born in March on the very first day. She was beautiful and marvelous in every way.

The right side of her face had a mark that was red. "It's a vascular birthmark," one of her doctor's said.

Rose's birthmark is called a port wine stain.
It does not wash off in the bath or the rain.

The blood vessels right under the skin are bigger and allow more blood to get in. This makes the area look different for sure. It stays more reddened than the rest of her.

It becomes darker or lighter when she gets hot or cold.

It grows with her as she gets bigger and will be part of her even when she is old.

To keep her skin healthy, Rose visits a skin clinician. Her expert team has a nurse, nurse practitioner, and a physician.

A special laser light is used and leaves purple dots. It sometimes lightens her birthmark and keeps it from getting thick and bumpy in spots.

The purple dots are just bruises that fade over time, each one is about the size of a dime.

Instead of staring, pointing or asking what is "wrong" with her face, it is more kind when asked questions with a bit more grace.

You see, nothing is "wrong" with the face of sweet Rose. She is made marvelous from her head to her toes.

Rose looks somewhat different than other kids do, but inside she is a lot like the rest of you.

She loves to play, have fun, swim, and run.

And has to be careful to protect her skin from the sun.

Our world is full of things that aren't the same. It keeps it from being boring and lame.

All sorts of books and music appeal to different minds. An assortment of sports and candy allow us to have favorites of varying kinds.

Some people are short and some are tall. Our skin, hair, and eyes aren't the same colors at all!

Ice cream is more tasty because there are flavors galore.

Chocolate, strawberry, mint, cotton candy, and more!

Imagine if you went on a trip to the zoo...

Isn´t it more fun to see tall giraffes munching on leaves...

Difference is good, it makes us unique and cool.

It reflects who you are and makes
you precious like a jewel.

Rose's birthmark is a part of her, whether it is dark or light. She wears it proudly and loves herself and others with might.

So, when you see someone who looks different than you, say "hello" and remember to share a big smile, too.

Kindness is the best gift you can give.

It leaves a lasting imprint on this world where we live.

By reading this story, hopefully you know, you are made marvelous, just like sweet Rose!

I will praise thee; for I am fearfully and wonderfully made: marvellous are thy works; and that my soul knoweth right well.
Psalm 139:14 KJV

MORE THAN A BIRTHMARK

Do you have a birthmark? Where is it? What does it look like? Do you love it, hate it, cover it up or wear it proudly? Did you know that approximately 1 in 10 children are born with a vascular birthmark of some sort? In fact, 3 out of every 1,000 children are diagnosed with a Port Wine Stain (PWS) birthmark specifically. Our daughter, Rose, was born with a PWS birthmark on the right side of her face and scalp. We have done hours of research and sought opinions from multiple medical experts in order to make the best educated decisions for her care and for her future.

Port wine stains are more than just birthmarks. They are not hereditary and have not been linked to any cause. PWS result directly from a somatic gene mutation occurring within the first few weeks of gestation. They do not regress on their own and actually grow in proportion with the child. The birthmark or coloring itself is caused by abnormal blood vessels below the skin that stay dilated which allow more blood to flow to the affected area. If left untreated, 70% of PWS thicken in response to tissue overgrowth and can have complications such as asymmetry, nodules and bleeding. Most PWS occur on the face, however, can occur on other parts of the body and can also be associated with vascular malformations on organs other than the skin. A rare, neurological disorder, known as Sturge-Weber Syndrome, can also occur as a result of a vascular malformation being present on the brain.

The recommended treatment for PWS is laser therapy using a specific laser called a pulsed dye laser (PDL). The laser light passes through the skin and is absorbed by the hemoglobin in the dilated vessels. The heat within the vessels causes damage to the vessel walls and often leaves bruising called purpura that resembles purple dots. The intensity of the purpura varies with each treatment depending on the settings used, the individual being treated, and the amount of abnormal blood vessels effectively targeted by the laser. The purpura fades on its own after 2-3 weeks. It is recommended that laser therapy be started as early in infancy or young childhood as possible due to treatment being more effective on younger skin. The ultimate goal of treatment is to keep the skin healthy and prevent thickening of the skin and other complications in the future. Laser treatments also cause lightening of the port wine stain which can help with some of the psychological effects that accompany having an obvious physical difference. The degree of lightening and the frequency of treatments needed varies greatly with each individual.

This journey has taught us many things. We have learned extensively about vascular birthmarks, experienced the importance of being our daughter's advocate in multiple settings, gained compassion and empathy as healthcare providers and are grateful for where we are today and those we have met along the path. We hope to use our experience with Rose as a platform to educate others about Port Wine Stains and to help our daughter make her mark on the world in which we live. What will your mark be?

10 FACTS ABOUT PORT WINE STAINS

1. Are always present at birth
2. Very, very rarely fade out naturally
3. Respond best to pulse dye laser treatment
4. Occur equally in males to females
5. A GNAQ gene mutation has been identified in PWS
6. PWS can be associated with Sturge Weber Syndrome
7. Most commonly occur in the head and neck
8. Are progressive lesions
9. Can thicken and cause cobbling with some PWS as they age
10. Can result in maximum clearance if treated early and frequently (Done by One)

www.birthmark.org

*Fact sheet created by Dr. Linda Rozell-Shannon, PhD, President/Founder of The Vascular Birthmarks Foundation and adapted for use with author's permission. The Vascular Birthmarks Foundation (VBF) works as a resource for families to make sure they are educated about their options and to assist in networking to find treatment needs.

www.ingramcontent.com/pod-product-compliance
Lightning Source LLC
Chambersburg PA
CBHW041124070526
44584CB00003B/274